HERALDIC DESIGNS

ARTHUR CHARLES
FOX-DAVIES

INTRODUCTION BY

JOHN P. B. BROOKE-LITTLE

NORROY AND ULSTER KING OF ARMS

BRACKEN BOOKS
LONDON

PUBLISHED BY BRACKEN BOOKS
A DIVISION OF BESTSELLER PUBLICATIONS LTD
PRINCESS HOUSE
50 EASTCASTLE STREET
LONDON W1N 7AP
ENGLAND

HERALDIC DESIGNS
IS A SELECTION OF PLATES FROM
THE ART OF HERALDRY – AN ENCYCLOPEDIA OF ARMORY
BY ARTHUR CHARLES FOX-DAVIES
ORIGINALLY PUBLISHED, 1904
REPUBLISHED BLOOMSBURY BOOKS, 1986

POSTER ART SERIES

HERALDIC DESIGNS
IS A VOLUME IN THE BRACKEN POSTER ART
SERIES. UP TO TEN PLATES MAY BE
REPRODUCED IN ANY ONE PROJECT OR
PUBLICATION, WITHOUT SPECIAL PERMISSION
AND FREE OF CHARGE. WHEREVER POSSIBLE THE
AUTHOR, TITLE AND PUBLISHER SHOULD BE ACKNOWLEDGED
IN A CREDIT NOTE. FOR PERMISSION TO MAKE MORE EXTENSIVE USE
OF THE PLATES IN THIS BOOK APPLICATION
MUST BE MADE TO THE PUBLISHER.

ISBN 1 85170 172 9
PRINTED IN ITALY

INTRODUCTION

The real definition of heraldry, the first in the *Shorter Oxford English Dictionary*, is everything that a herald does in his professional capacity. He is concerned with ceremonial and precedence, with making proclamations, with tracing family history, but primarily with the design of coats of arms and recording and advising upon them. It is because the principal business of a herald has for centuries been centred on coats of arms that the study of these hereditary devices is popularly termed heraldry. For the sake of simplicity I shall use this definition, never losing sight of the fact that heralds have wider interests.

I have begged the questions, what are heralds and how did they come into being? Heralds were originally messengers and announcers, a cross between the first-class post and a newscaster. Think of 'Hark! The Herald Angels sing!' and think no more. The remote ancestors of modern heralds are to be found in the Bible, in classical fact and legend and in most ancient civilizations, but their immediate predecessors in England were the heralds who were attached to the Norman Court when the English were overcome by William, later called 'The Conqueror', in 1066. The heralds, at this time, were messengers and ceremonial officers and it was they who organized the jousts and tournaments, the mock battles of the period.

Even before the beginning of the twelfth century, it had become customary for the knights and nobles to paint devices on their shields. These were purely decorative, but perhaps the heralds saw that if the decoration of the shields were systematized and each knight used an unique and distinctive shield, it would enable everyone, and the heralds in particular, to recognize who was who.

By the beginning of the thirteenth century the heralds appear to have developed a system which was universally adopted by the Norman aristocracy. From which time onwards the royal heralds came to have control of the system; it became their principal concern.

One of the chief evidences for the early development of heraldry is the rolls of arms compiled by the heralds. Plate 1 depicts one of the earliest collections of arms, that which illustrates Matthew Paris's *Historia Anglorum* (1250 to 1259). Other rolls and books of arms of later date are depicted in plates 2, 3, 4, 5, 6, 7 and 8. Another important source of evidence is the use of arms from an early date on seals. In days of widespread illiteracy the nobles authenticated their documents not by signing them but by affixing their seals to them, so what better way of identifying the owner of a seal than by engraving his arms upon it? Some seals are shown in plate 9.

Symbolism is as old as humanity, so what makes heraldic symbolism unique? The answer is that it conforms to certain criteria. These may be categorized thus: the principal vehicle for the display of arms is the shield; the way in which devices are displayed upon a shield follows certain rules and conventions aimed at making the arms at once easily recognizable, attractive and symbolic; arms are hereditary in character, passing to all legitimate male descendants of the man to whom the arms were first granted or allowed and to his daughters until they marry; younger sons add differences to their arms to distinguish them from the head of the family (some are illustrated in plate 10); and finally, arms are in the nature of an honour, being ensigns of nobility and gentility. Being an honour they stem from the Crown, which, for centuries, has delegated the power of granting and controlling the bearing of arms to the senior heralds, called Kings of Arms.

Almost everything in life start by being simple, basic and utilitarian, and then gradually becomes more and more complicated; the growth of heraldry is no exception. At first there were shields of arms, often called coats of arms as they were also depicted on the bearer's surcoat, which he wore over his armour. Then, towards the end of the thirteenth century a subsidiary hereditary emblem called a crest became popular. This was a device modelled on top of the helm (plate 11 shows knights with crested helms, arms and surcoats); consequently when arms were depicted decoratively (as in plate 12), the crest was shown modelled onto the helm to which the mantling was also affixed. This latter was a short cloak, which some think was intended to shade the back of the helm from the sun, others to deaden sword blows to the neck, while yet others believe it to have been no more than a male conceit. Be that as it may, heraldic artists down the ages have been grateful for the existence of the mantling, as they use it in fantastic and impossible ways (hence the untutored often refer to it as 'foliage' or 'sea-weed') to make a good picture. Examples are to be found in plates 13, 14, 15 and in many of the other illustrations in this volume.

The introduction of the crest is by no means the end of the story. In the late fifteenth and during the sixteenth century the greater nobles added yet more complications to their arms, namely supporters. These consist of two creatures, human, or otherwise, who stand on either side of the shield, and literally support it. The origin of supporters is purely artistic. The importance of the individual was reflected in the size of the circumference of his seal. This gave the engravers of such seals sufficient space on either side of the arms to fill with decoration, as the more complex the design of a seal the more difficult it was to forge. Many engravers elected to fill this space with creatures which had some association with the family, possibly in its arms, crest or badges. In this way supporters were born and it was not long before the heralds considered them to be part of the armorial ensigns and so took them under their ample wings and made rules and regulations as to who should and who should not be entitled to bear them. The principal category of those who may bear supporters to their arms are peers of the realm. Plate 16 depicts the arms, with helmet, crest, mantling and supporters, of John Campbell (Gordon), 7th Earl of Aberdeen, G.C.M.G., later a Knight of the Thistle and first Marquess of Aberdeen and Temair.

This picture also demonstrates two more accretions to a full coat of arms (the technical name is achievement of arms), namely the motto and insignia, such as that of the Order of St Michael and St George and the coronet of an earl placed above the shield. The insignia are, of course, personal to the bearer of the arms and are in no way hereditary. On the other hand, the supporters are inherited, but only by the holder of the title.

Today, most families sport a motto, but before the late sixteenth century this was not usual, except in the case of some very noble families. Other achievements of arms of peers of the realm are illustrated in plate 17.

Although, as has been shown, heraldry originally served a practical purpose, its wider application was appreciated from the time of its inception. Its use on seals has already been noted, but, from very early days, it was also used commemoratively on tombs and brasses, in stained glass and, in fact, anywhere where a coat of arms could proclaim its owner's presence, or mark his property. Today arms are still used on book-plates, stationery, porcelain, silver, flags, motor cars, and other personal possessions, such as hair brushes, cuff-links, brooches and so forth. If the uses of heraldry had not been extended beyond the narrow confines of the battlefield and tournament ground, it would not have survived the fifteenth century and so flourished today. Some uses of heraldry are illustrated in plate 18 (Swiss stained glass windows), plate 19 (porcelain) and plate 20 which depicts an armorial flag called a banner.

Another reason why heraldry survived the Middle Ages and is still very much a living art and science is because since the fourteenth century corporate bodies have used arms in much the same way as individuals. To understand how this came about it is necessary to view heraldry in its widest perspective, to see it as a form of symbolism stemming from the Crown and so being a matter of legitimate pride to individuals and their families. After all, a corporate body is really only a large group or clan and as such is in need of a symbol upon which can be focused the loyalty and pride of its members. What then could be more natural than for a corporation to come to the Kings of Arms and supplicate for devices to be granted to it in the form of arms duly recorded and protected?

So, from early times, bishoprics had arms (plate 21) as did cities, towns and other municipalities (plate 22) and corporations such as Trade Guilds or Livery Companies, Masonic Lodges (plate 23) and, more recently, banks, insurance companies, airlines, colleges, commercial corporations, professional bodies, and hospitals. The list is endless, but, in all cases, the recipients of grants of arms are worthy corporations which serve the community in their various ways.

The development of heraldry over the centuries has been briefly noted, but the heralds, who were responsible for all that happened, have so far been left out of the account. Let me now trace their evolution. Soon there emerged three degrees or ranks of herald: there were the junior officers, at first the apprentices, who were called Pursuivants; next the Heralds (with a capital H, as the word herald is used both generically for all degrees of herald and specifically for the middle rank), and finally the Kings of Arms, who had, as has been noted, armorial jurisdiction.

Heraldry developed in slightly different ways in the various European countries, but everywhere its development and control were monitored by heralds, who wore their master's surcoat or tabard as their distinctive uniform (see plates 26, 27 and 28). Here I am going to consider briefly the history of the English heralds because they still form a very active body exercising an imperial jurisdiction within the Commonwealth.

By the early fourteenth century, it was customary for Pursuivants, Heralds and Kings of Arms to be given names or titles. The English royal heralds today have titles which go back for hundreds of years. The four Pursuivants are called Rouge Dragon, Rouge Croix, Portcullis and Blue-mantle. The six Heralds are Windsor, Richmond, Somerset, Chester, Lan-caster and York. For heraldic purposes England is divided by the river Trent into two provinces. Each province is ruled over, heraldically speaking, by a King of Arms; Clarenceux has jurisdiction south of the Trent, and Norroy and Ulster north of that river and in Northern Ireland. Finally, there is a senior king, named Garter, who does not have a province but is, as it were, chairman of the heralds and an officer of the Order of the Garter.

In 1484 King Richard III incorporated the royal heralds and gave them a residence in London. They were reincorporated in 1555 and the corporation, known as the College of Arms, is to be found in Queen Victoria Street in the City of London. Here, the heraldic and genealogical records are kept and the heralds have their chambers, acting for the public in matters of heraldry and also compiling family trees, such as the rather elaborate examples depicted in plates 24 and 25.

Here I should perhaps mention that the royal heraldry emblazoned on the tabards illustrated differs from family heraldry in that the arms used by sovereigns are not necessarily their family arms, but those of sovereignty or dominion. They are, therefore, akin to corporate rather than personal arms. Some royal coats are illustrated in plate 29 and the symbolic crowns of some European monarchies are depicted in plate 30. Many of these are based on the actual crowns used, such as the famous Hungarian Crown of St Stephen (fig. 4), while others, such as the German Imperial Crown (fig. 2) never actually existed.

Heraldry is an European and Christian phenomenon, deriving much of its early impetus from the Crusades, when all the knights of Christendom met and joined together to defend the Holy Places from the infidel. But, as might be expected, it developed differently in each country, so that whilst the basic framework of heraldic practice did not vary greatly, it grew and flourished in a variety of different ways. For example, compare the Hungarian and Polish arms shown in plate 31 with the French arms in plates 32 and 33 and the Austrian sixteenth and seventeenth century arms in plates 34 and 35. It will at once be apparent that there are both similarities and differences between them.

It is not always appreciated what limitations are placed upon an heraldic artist or how much freedom he has to render a coat of arms in any number of different ways. Essentially, the objects in the arms, crest and supporters, their disposition and their colours must not be altered. The position of the helm and the colours of the mantling are also fixed, but beyond this the artist is free to use whatever type of shield and helm he pleases, to design the mantling as he chooses and to a certain extent to select the shades of colour which he employs. For example, the arms of Cullen, illustrated in plate 36, could quite properly be shown on any of the many types of shield depicted in plate 37.

Some people are put off by what is often termed heraldic jargon, while others find in it the fascination of the esoteric. In fact, it is neither particularly difficult to master, nor in any way secret or obscure. It is simply a way of describing arms in a terse and unequivocal manner. The reason it seems obscure at first is because many of the words are taken from the Norman French, for that was the language of the English Court until the end of the thirteenth century and beyond. To describe arms in heraldic terms is to blazon them, blazon being based on a number of rules or conventions. It would be impossible to detail all the rules of blazon here, but let me just give one example, which I hope will serve to demonstrate the basis of blazon. The arms of Cullen, referred to above and illustrated in plate 36, are blazoned: Or, an eagle displayed sable, beaked and membered gules.

The background of the shield is called the field and this is always described first in a blazon. Here it is Or, which is the term used for gold and comes from the French. There is no need to say 'the field is gold' as this is assumed by the use of the one word 'Or'. Next the principal charge is mentioned. The symbols and objects used in heraldry are called charges, and some of the basic geometrical charges are shown in plate 38 and others in plate 39. Here there is only one charge, an eagle displayed. By stating that it is displayed, it is understood that it will be shown with wings outspread and the head turned to look towards the right hand side of the shield; a shield is always described as if it were being carried, so right (dexter) becomes left (sinister) and vice versa. In the French fashion the adjectives describing a noun are placed after it, so its colour, Sable, is detailed next. Sable is the heraldic term used for black. 'Beaked and membered gules' indicates that the beak and claws are red (gules being a word of obscure origin meaning red) although strictly speaking the term 'membered' should also refer to the legs.

I need not elaborate on the visual attraction of heraldry as the plates do that far more eloquently than I can, but I hope I have managed to show that behind the colourful designs there lies a wealth of history and a whole new and exciting science to explore. For he who accepts the challenge the rewards can be varied and infinite.

John P. B. Brooke-Little, C.V.O., M.A., F.S.A.
Norroy and Ulster King of Arms
Heyford House
January 1988

ARMS.
Drawn by Matthew Paris, &c.

PLATE 1

Arms drawn by Matthew Paris (d. 1259) from the Historia Anglorum *(1250–1259)*

Some of the earliest drawings of arms by the famous artist Matthew Paris who played an important role in thirteenth century society, not only as a scholar and historian, but also as the confidant and advisor to some of the crowned heads of Europe. Heraldic representations in his many works are for the most part executed by himself, and are some of the best examples of illumination in this period. Above the shields in this plate stand the names of the respective owners of the arms. The most notable are:

Fig 1. Frederick II, Roman Emperor

Fig 2. St Louis IX, King of France

Fig 3. Alexander II, King of Scotland

Fig 8. Richard, Earl of Cornwall and Poitou (died 1272)

Fig 9. Simon de Montfort, Earl of Leicester, High Steward of England (died 1265)

Fig 14. Earl of Chester. These arms are still used and attributed to the Earldom of Chester

Fig 15. Raimund, Count of Toulouse who was the brother-in-law of King John

EXAMPLES FROM THE ZURICH "WAPPENROLLE."

PLATE 2

Examples from the Züricher Wappenrolle
(*first half of the fourteenth century*)

*This register is the oldest German collection
of arms and in its original condition con-
tained 559 coats of arms and 28 episcopal
banners*

Fig 5. Betler (meaning beggar)

*Fig 6. Habsburg. This is the earliest coat
of arms of the Counts von Habsburg
– dating from 1186*

ARMS FROM GELRE'S "WAPENBOECK."

PLATE 3

Arms from Gelre's Wapenboeck (*probably circa 1370*)

This work by Claes Heynen, Gelre Herald 1334–1372) contains about 1800 hand-coloured representations of coats of arms

Fig 1. King Pedro II (the Cruel) of Spain (died 1369)

Fig 3. The Earl of Moray

Fig 5. King Charles II (the Bad) of Navarre (died 1387)

Fig 10. Sir Alexander Stewart of Buchan and Badenoch (died 1404)

Fig 11. Lord Seton

Fig 12. Annandale, properly the arms of Bruce, Lords of Annandale, Scotland

Fig 14. The King of Cyprus

Fig 15. De Vere, Earls of Oxford

ARMS FROM HERALDIC BOOKS OF XV. CENTURY.

PLATE 4

Arms from Heraldic books (fifteenth century)

Fig 1. Holy Roman German Empire, from the Handregistratur *of King Frederick IV*

Figs 2–4. Taken from the Oesterreichisches Wappenbuch (*Austrian Book of Arms*)

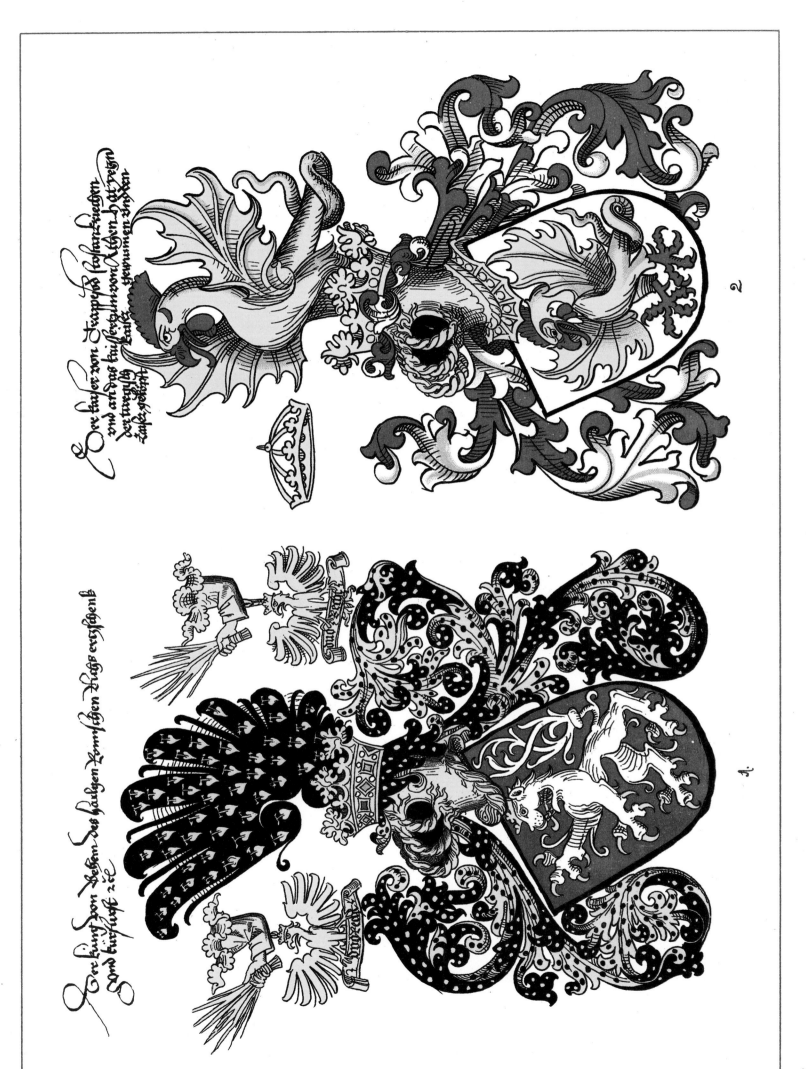

EXAMPLES FROM CONRAD GRUNENBERG'S WAPPENBUCH.

Herrn von Berxo

Hey Her von Zimern vnd
Here   zuo Mosßkirch
vmt   vm   vlch

do
Heren haffendoff

1.

2.

3.

Von langenstain flister
des tutschen huses der Maynß

Von Rottenstam
Lud von
buttmen

Von frankenstain

Nch stifter zr haur
vnßan

4.

5.

6.

7.

monßz water
ffanconberge

Le seigneur
de Welles

Monßz Richard
de Shizbnzne

Sir James
Hrangweys

lef de shastade
halghton

le sð De
Anerleton

Comes de
Seyne

Sir John
Apseley

attewater

frier an Roy

☩ Dykot

Robert
thorne

The emperour

Coche

Judde

dantrey

ARMS FROM "PRINCE ARTHUR'S BOOK."

PLATE 7

Arms from Prince Arthur's Book (*1501–1502*)

Tradition has it that this book was expressly made for the purposes of teaching the laws of armory together with the arms in use in England to Arthur, Prince of Wales, the eldest son of King Henry VII, however most of the book is of later date. The arms of most families of importance in England and many of the principal personages of Europe are duly emblazoned in the volume. This plate represents a series of shields selected as typical of those throughout the volume

The armes oft the Realme oft france

Duc de york

the lord thomas wulsey cardinal legat de latere archebisshop oft yorke and chancelor oft Jngland

Dockwra

DESIGNS FROM "PRINCE ARTHUR'S BOOK."

PLATE 8

Further examples from Prince Arthur's Book (*1501–1502*)

These examples represent a curious decorative development of heraldry in Tudor times: the supporters, which are represented singly, are each depicted supporting a banner. In many cases, however, they are really family beasts rather than official supporters, and some of the banners depict badges rather than arms

Top Left. *The Realm of France*

Top Right. *The badge of the Duke of York – later Edward IV*

Bottom Left. *Cardinal Wolsey, Legate de Latere, Archbishop of York, and Chancellor of England*

Bottom Right. *Sir Thomas Dockwra, Prior of the English Priory of the Knights of St John*

HERALDIC AND OTHER SEALS.

PLATE 9

Specimens of Armorial and other Seals
From the birth of heraldry arms have been
frequently used on seals

Fig 1. Ferdinand I, as King of Hungary
(1526–1564)

Fig 2. Albert Baron (Freiherr) von
Winkel, Bishop of Passau (1363–
1380)

Fig 3. Lancelot Blackbourne, Bishop of
Exeter (1716–1724)

Fig 4. Lazar Brankovies of Servia
reproduced from a document dated
1457

Fig 5. Leonhard von Keutschach,
Archbishop of Salzburg (1495–
1519)

Fig 6. Maximilian Gandolf, Archbishop
of Salzburg, Count von Khuenburg
(1668–1687)

Fig 7. Great Seal of the Swiss Canton of
Berne

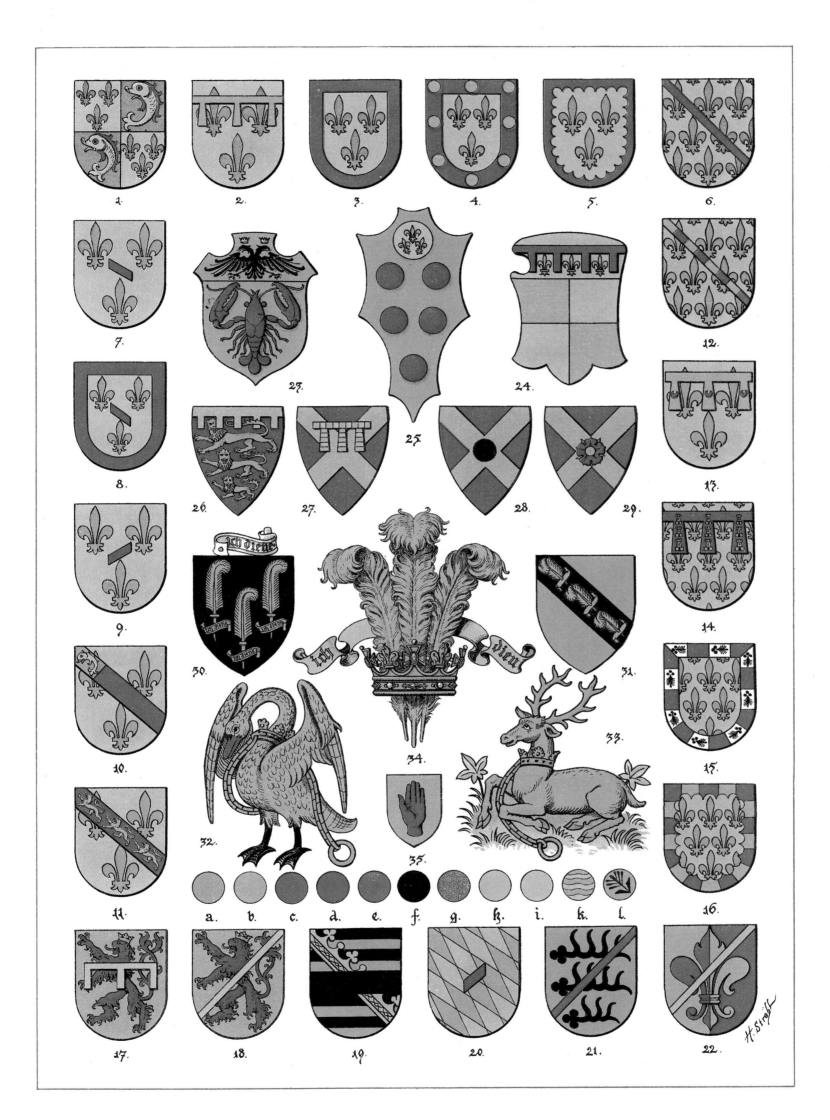

EXAMPLES OF "DIFFERENCED" COATS OF ARMS, &c.

PLATE 10

Examples of 'Differenced' Coats of Arms
Various systems of 'differencing' developed
throughout Europe as a means of distinguish-
ing the armorial bearings of younger male
members from those of the head of a family.
In England there are no difference marks
whatsoever for daughters, there being in
English law no seniority between the daughters
of one man; nor are there marks of difference
between illegitimate children

1.   2.

3.   4.

TOURNAMENT EQUESTRIAN FIGURES.

PLATE 11

Tournament Equestrian Figures

Armorial insignia were actually worn and carried in battle or tournament. These figures taken from Tournament Rolls show the customary array for those taking part – crested helms, arms and surcoats. The upper group shows:

Fig 1. The Duke of Brittany

Fig 2. The Duke of Bourbon

The lower groups shows two German knights:

Fig 3. Wolmershausen

Fig 4. A knight from the Rhineland

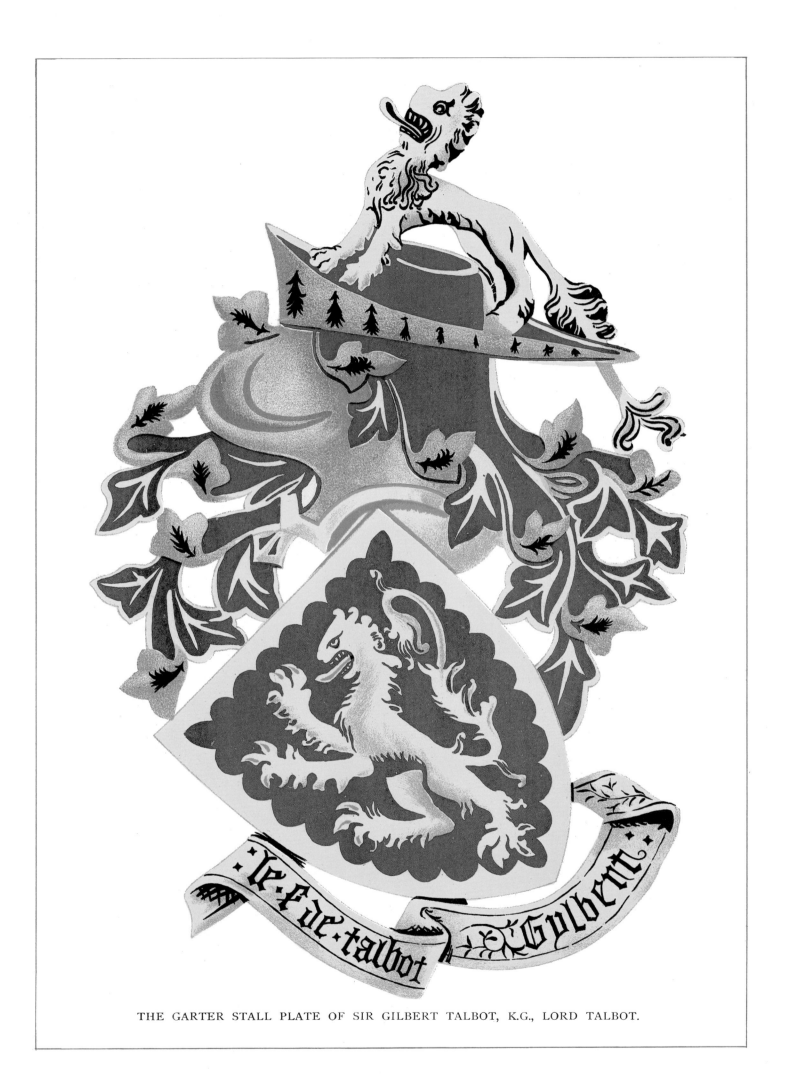

THE GARTER STALL PLATE OF SIR GILBERT TALBOT, K.G., LORD TALBOT.

PLATE 12

The Garter Stall plate of Sir Gilbert Talbot, K.G., 5th Lord Talbot

These decorative arms are an example from one of the most important series of English armorial designs, the Stall plates of the Knights of the Garter in St George's Chapel, Windsor Castle. The Order of the Garter was founded in 1348, and at this date one of the chapels of Windsor Castle was fitted up for the order, wherein have been placed the helmet, crest and sword of every knight. Many of the plates of the founder knights still remain, and of the eight hundred or more knights who have since been appointed to the order, very nearly six hundred Stall plates remain

THE ARMORIAL BEARINGS OF —

(1) J. W. MELLES, Esq. of Gruline, Aros, Isle of Mull.
(2) Sir THOMAS WRIGHT, of Leicester.
(3) EDWARD THOMAS TYSON, Esq. of Wood Hall, Cockermouth.

(4) HERBERT LUSHINGTON STOREY, Esq., of Lancaster.
(5) HOWEL J. J. PRICE, Esq. of Greensted Hall, Ongar.

PLATE 13

The Armorial Bearings of:

Fig 1. W. Melles, Esq. of Gruline, Aros, Isle of Mull

Fig 2. Sir Thomas Wright of Leicester

Fig 3. Edward Thomas Tyson, Esq. of Wood Hall, Cockermouth

Fig 4. Herbert Lushington Storey, Esq. of Lancaster

Fig 5. Howel J. J. Price, Esq. of Greenstead Hall, Ongar

Free for a blast

Amat victoria curam

Sub spe

FY·NUW·FY·NGWLAD·A'I·GWYRTHIAU

TURRIS·TUTISSIMA·VIRTUS

PLATE 14

The Armorial Bearings of:

Fig 1. Lt.-Col. Robert Mildmay, Clerk of Westholme, Co. Somerset

Fig 2. Rev. John Archibald Dunbar-Dunbar of Sea Park, Forres

Fig 3. Mayor E. Uvedale Price

Fig 4. Eyton

Fig 5. T. A. Carlyon, Esq. of Boscombe Park, Bournemouth

THE ARMORIAL BEARINGS OF—

(1) JOHN ALEXANDER GALBRAITH, Esq
(2) MATTHEW WILSON HERVEY, Esq.
(3) FRANCIS JAMES GRANT, Esq., Rothesay Herald and Lyon Clerk.

(4) ALBEMARLE O'BEIRNE WILLOUGHBY DEWAR, Esq. of "Doles" Hants.
(5) REGINALD HENRY TUDOR DRUMMOND, Esq. of Balquhandy.

PLATE 16

The Armorial Bearings of John Campbell (Gordon), 7th Earl of Aberdeen G.C.M.G.

As a Peer of the Realm (later a Knight of the Thistle and first Marquess of Aberdeen and Temair) John Campbell (Gordon) was entitled to bear supporters to his arms. These are: dexter an Earl and sinister a Doctor of Laws, both in their robes all proper

LOYAL A MORT

PRENDS·MOI·TEL·QUE·JE·SUIS·

TIEN TA FOY

LIKEM CHOICE

LABORE·ET·CONSILIO·

PLATE 17

Achievements of Arms of Peers of the Realm

Although common today, before the late sixteenth century only very noble families would sport a motto. In England these are not hereditary, no-one is compelled to bear one, nor is any authority needed for their adoption. The matter is left purely to the personal pleasure of every person, as is the position in which the motto is to be carried and the manner in which it is to be displayed

Fig 1. Marquess of Ely

Fig 2. Seymour, 7th Earl Bathurst and his wife Hon. Lilian Borthwick

Fig 3. Viscount Halifax

Fig 4. Lord Rendel

2.

1.

PLATE 18

Examples of Swiss Heraldic windows (six-teenth century)

The essentially Swiss custom of presenting windows as ceremonial gifts gave rise in the sixteenth century to a huge upsurge in the art of glass-painting

Fig 1. The arms of von Lüttishofen, a noble family resident in the Cantons of Zürich and Lucerne

Fig 2. The arms of Peter Ritter von Engelsberg

ARMORIAL DESIGNS FOR PORCELAIN.

DESIGN FOR A TALBOT BANNER.

PLATE 20

Design for a Talbot banner (early fifteenth century)

Armorial flags, called banners, probably developed from heraldic badge designs. The armorial use of the banner in connection with the display of heraldic achievements is very limited in this country. The manner of their depiction is generally determined purely on aesthetic grounds. This example shows one of a series of banner designs prepared for the Talbot family, Earls of Shrewsbury

EXAMPLES OF ECCLESIASTICAL HERALDRY.

PLATE 21

Examples of Ecclesiastical Heraldry

In all European countries ecclesiastical heraldry has an important place in armorial matters. The ecclesiastical hat affords one of the few instances where the rules governing heraldic usage are almost identical throughout the continent

Fig 1. His Holiness the late Pope Leo XIII (Joachim Pecci) 1810–1903

Fig 3. Cardinals – a red hat with fifteen tassels on each side

Fig 4. Patriarchs – a green hat with fifteen green tassels on each side, the cords and fiocci interwoven with gold

Fig 6. Archbishops – a green hat with ten green tassels on each side

Fig 10. Bishops (of the Roman Church) – a green hat with six green tassels on each side

Fig 18. Mitred Abbots and Provosts – a black hat with three black tassels on each side

COATS OF ARMS OF TOWNS.

PAINTED PANEL IN THE POSSESSION OF
W. HY RYLANDS, *circa 1680.*

BANNER IN THE POSSESSION OF THE LODGE
OF YORK. *circa 1779.*

HOLINESS TO THE LORD

Arms of the
CITY OF COLOGNE.

STONE MASONS OF STRASBURG.
from seal circa 1725.

STONE MASONS OF NURENBURG.
from seal circa 1725.

The arms borne by
GRAND LODGE OF ALL ENGLAND.
circa 1725.

IN GOD IS AL OVR TRVST

BRICKLAYERS AND TILERS.
from Gateshead charter 1671.

MASONS OF COLOGNE.
from seal 1396 (colours restored)

ARMS OF MASONIC AND KINDRED BODIES.

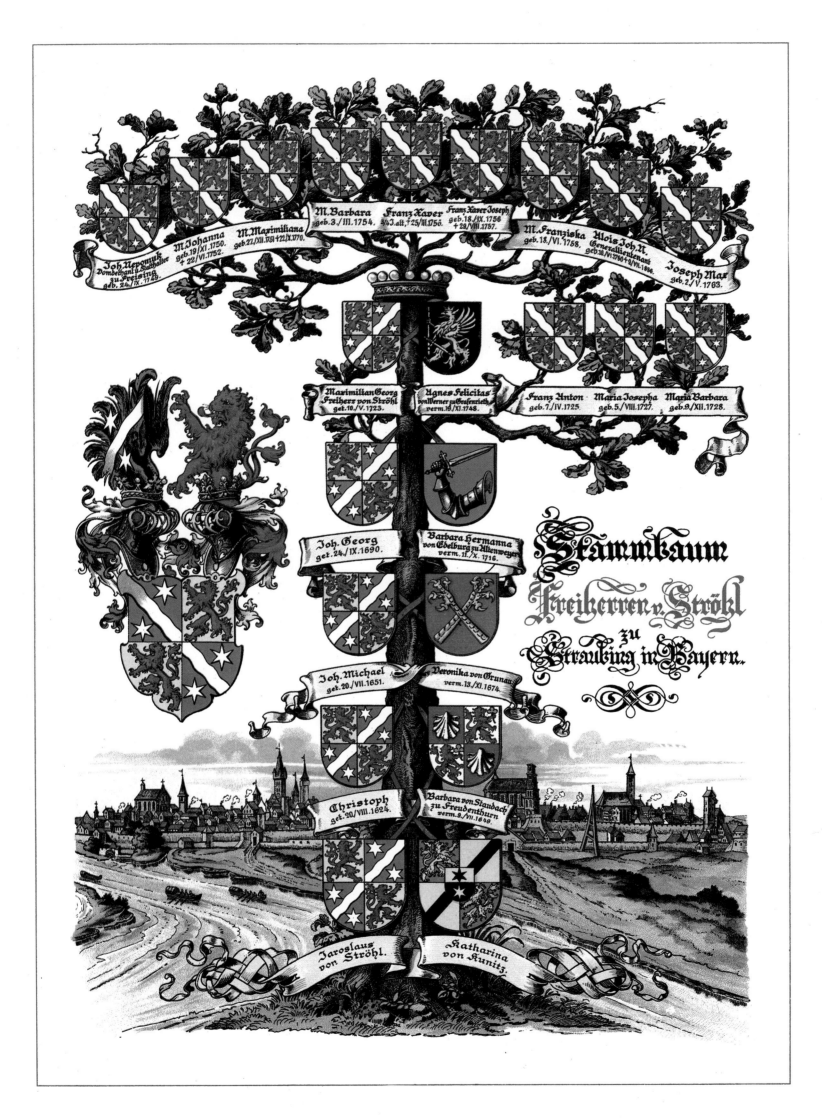

AN EXAMPLE OF AN ILLUMINATED GENEALOGICAL TREE.

PLATE 24

An Example of an Illuminated Genealogical Tree. The Pedigree of Ströhl

This family, which became extinct on the death of the Bavarian Lieutenant-General Alois, Freiherr von Ströhl, in the year 1836, was supposed to have originally owned estates in Silesia and in Lausitz, and to have borne the name of Strela or Strel. At the foot of the family tree, as the first authentically proved bearer of the noble name of Ströhl, is Jaroslaus, married to Katharina von Kunitz

AN EXAMPLE OF AN ILLUMINATED PROOF OF SEIZE QUARTIERS.

An Example of an Illuminated proof of
Seize-Quartiers

Seize-Quartiers *is a widely misunderstood and misused term. It may only properly be claimed when a person can show that all sixteen great-great-grandparents were in their own right entitled to bear arms*

MARCH PURSUIVANT OF ARMS.

PLATE 26

George Swinton, March Pursuivant of Arms
(1901–1923)

The Scottish Heralds each have a rod of ebony tipped with ivory, which is sometimes stated to be a rod of office. This, however, is not the case and the explanation of it is very simple: they are constantly called upon to make the Royal Proclamations from the Market Cross in Edinburgh. These are read from printed copies which in terms of type and paper are always of the nature of a poster. The Herald would naturally find some difficulty in holding up a large piece of paper of this size, consequently he winds it round his ebony staff, slowly unwinding it all the time as he reads. Captain Swinton, March Pursuivant, is here shown wearing white knee-breeches and hose, the appropriate dress for either a full state ceremony or a coronation

HERALDS IN OFFICIAL DRESS.

PLATE 27

Heralds in Official Dress

Fig 1. Claes Heynen, Gelre Herald (see plate 3)

Fig 2. A King of Arms (fifteenth century), possibly a herald of Louis de Bruges, Seigneur de Grutuse

Fig 3. The King of Arms of the Order of the Golden Fleece (mid-sixteenth century)

Fig 4. A German Imperial Herald (first half of the sixteenth century)

Fig 5. Caspar Sturm, appointed Imperial Herald in 1521, his title being Teutschland, meaning Germany

Fig 6. Johann von Francolin, the younger, Royal Hungarian Herald (1560)

Fig 7. Herald of Brandenburg, under the Great Elector, Frederick III (latter half of the seventeenth century)

PLATE 28

Heralds in Official Dress

These Heralds are of the eighteenth and nineteenth centuries

Fig 1. Arms of the English College of Arms

Fig 2. Garter King of Arms – in his tabard and full dress, the tabard showing the Royal Arms of the United Kingdom of Great Britain and Ireland

Fig 5. A Royal Bavarian Herald (1864)

Fig 6. A Bavarian Pursuivant

Fig 7. A Hungarian Provincial Herald (1867)

Fig 8. Herald of the Imperial Capital and City of Vienna

Fig 9. A Royal Swedish Herald (eighteenth century)

ARMS OF SOVEREIGNTY, DOMINION, &c.

PLATE 29

Arms of Sovereignty and Dominion

Royal arms are in many respects different from ordinary armorial bearings, and it should be carefully borne in mind that they stand not for any particular area of land, but for the intangible sovereignty vested in the rulers thereof. They are not necessarily, nor are they in fact, hereditary. They pass by conquest. Like other arms, however, differences are used by the younger members of the family

Fig 1. German Empire

Fig 2. Kingdom of Greece

Fig 3. Grand Duchy of Luxemburg

Fig 4. Kingdom of Ireland

Fig 6. Duchy of Salzburg

Fig 9. Swiss Canton of Uri

Fig 10. English town of Southampton (confirmed 1575)

Fig 13. Mon of the Empire of Japan

Fig 15. Kingdom of Siam

Fig 17. State of Maine, United States of North America

Fig 18. United Republic of Brazil

IMPERIAL AND ROYAL CROWNS OF EUROPE.

PLATE 30

Imperial and Royal Crowns of Europe

From the earliest times of recorded history, crowns have been a silent emblem of sovereignty. It is believed that they were originally worn by kings in battle in order that they might be easily recognized

Fig 1. Austrian Imperial Crown (1602)

Fig 2. German Imperial Crown

Fig 3. Russian Emperor's Crown (time of Empress Catherine II)

Fig 5. Crown of the German Empress

Fig 12. Italian Royal Crown

Fig 13. Austrian Archducal Crown or Cap

Fig 14. Crown of the Crown Prince of Sweden

Fig 15. Plevna Crown, the Royal Crown of Rumania

EXAMPLES OF HUNGARIAN AND POLISH ARMS.

PLATE 31

Examples of Hungarian and Polish Arms

While Hungarian heraldry rests more or less on a German foundation, and only makes itself noticeable by its occasional extravagances, ancient Polish heraldry would seem to be of an independent origin, possessing very little in common with German or West European heraldic art. Old Polish armorial devices are mostly the flag-devices, 'Stannizan', of the families of the old dynasties. These coats of arms were not borne by one family only, but in each case by a whole group of families who, however, would originate from the same dynasty

Figs 1–6. Hungarian Coats of Arms

Figs 7–8. Polish Coats of Arms

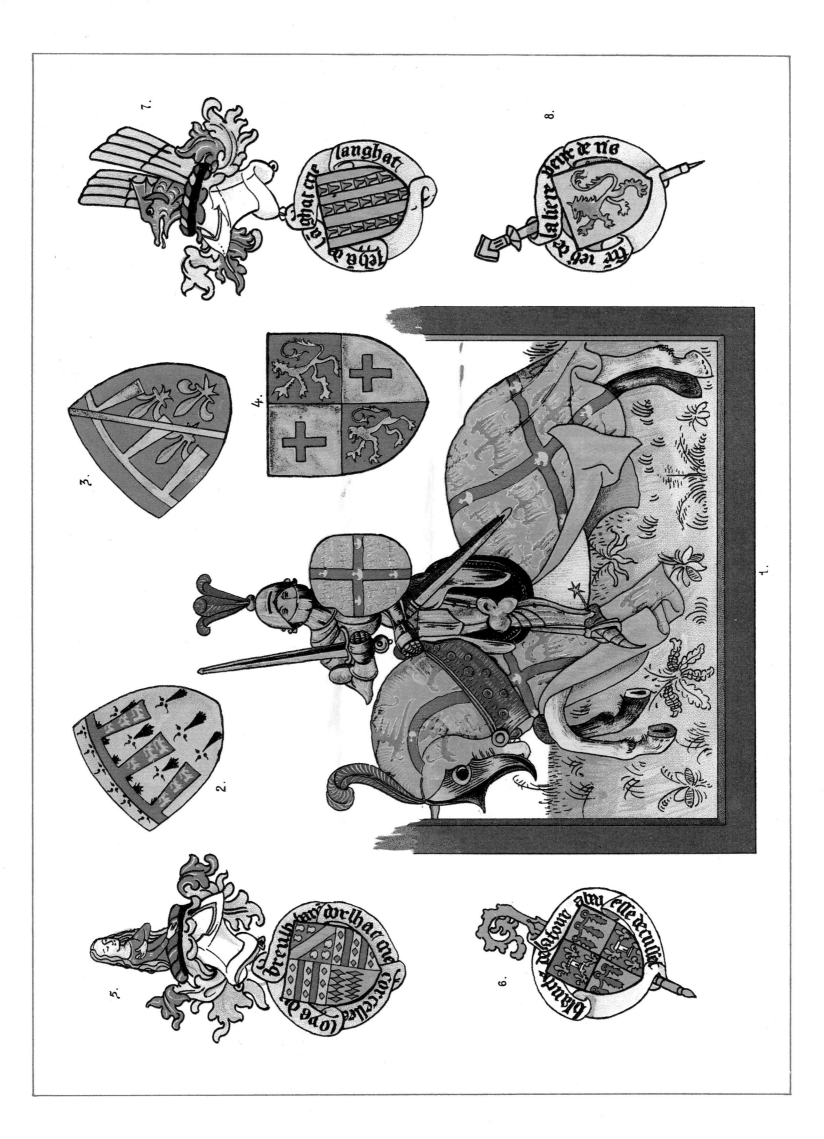

PLATE 32

Examples of French Heraldry (fifteenth century)

France has always been of considerable importance in matters of armory. French and particularly Burgundian heralds and Pursuivants had the reputation of being especially proficient. They transplanted French armorial usages and many of their technical words into German soil, without thereby stemming the national development of German heraldic art. In English terms of blazon the influence of France is apparent, though it is not unlikely that to the general usage of the Norman-French language, the 'French' terms should more correctly be attributed

Fig 1. Equestrian figure of one of the family of Montmorency-Laval, one of the oldest noble families in France

Fig 3. Armorial shield of Lieutenant-Général le comte de Donnois, bastard d'Orléans

Fig 6. Arms of Blanche de Latour, abbesse de Cusset

Fig 8. Arms of Brother Jehan de la Lière, Prior of Ris

EXAMPLES OF FRENCH HERALDRY.

PLATE 33

Examples of French Heraldry (seventeenth, eighteenth and early nineteenth centuries:

Fig 1. Achievement representing the alliance of King Henry IV of France and Marie de Medici in the chapel of the Château de Fontaine-bleau, of the time of Louis XIII (1610–1643)

Fig 2. Arms of Marie de Trémoille (Trémouille) from the time of Louis XIII

Fig 3. Arms of Maître François Elie de Voyer de Paulmy d'Argenson, at first Bishop of Dol, then Arch-bishop and Prince of Embrun, Count of Guillestre and of Beaufort (from a manuscript of 1698)

Fig 4. Arms of the Nicolay family (from a book of 1768)

Fig 5. Design for a regimental flag, with the arms of France and the arms of the Count de Noyon (1789)

Fig 6. Arms of Jean Domenique, Baron Larry, Inspector General of the Military Medicinal Staff

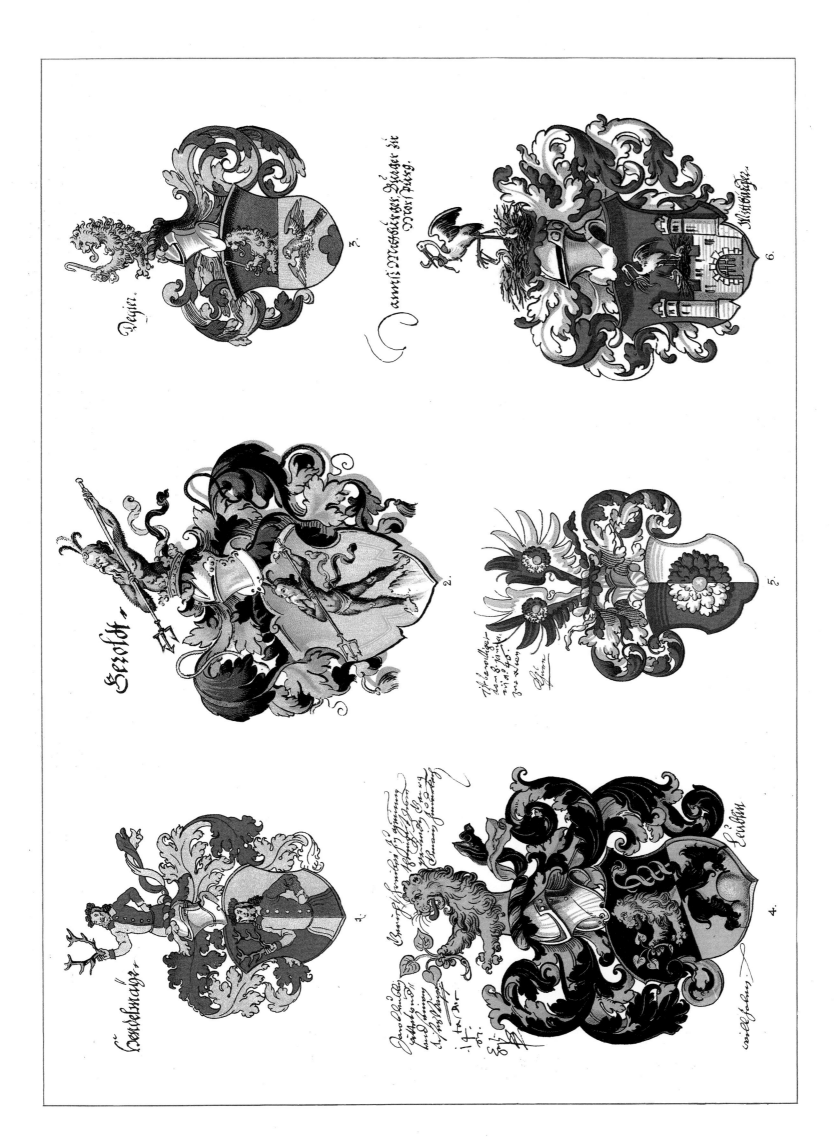

PLATE 34

Armorial Paintings (sixteenth century)

These examples are taken from a volume (Wappenbuch 1) in the Adelsarchiv (Nobility Archives) at Vienna. They are proposals for armorial designs drawn from old Government documents no longer in existence, and are annotated with critical remarks

Fig 1. Hendelmayr

Fig 2. Geroldt

Fig 3. Degier

Fig 4. Leublin

Fig 5. Khuen

Fig 6. Mittbürger

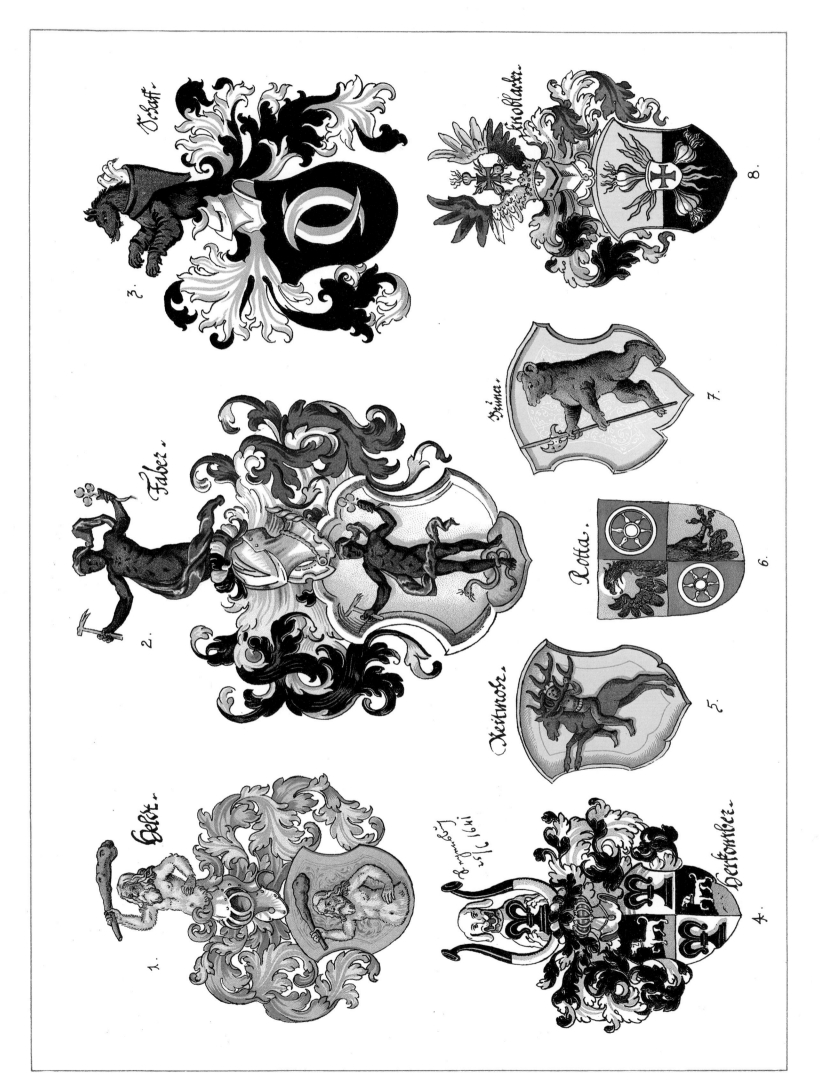

ARMORIAL PAINTINGS OF THE XVI. AND XVII. CENTURIES.

PLATE 35

Armorial Paintings (sixteenth and seven-teenth centuries)

These examples are drawn from Wappen-buch 2, *also in the Adelsarchiv in Vienna (see plate 34). They are not annotated, but a date of patent is recorded on the arms of Herkomber*

Fig 1. Heldt

Fig 2. Faber

Fig 3. Schaff

Fig 4. Herkomber

Fig 5. Reitmohr

Fig 6. Rotta

Fig 7. Bruner

Fig 8. Knoblacher

THE ARMS OF CULLEN.
Or, an eagle displayed sable, beaked and membered gules.
DESIGNED BY MISS C. HELARD.

PLATE 36
The Arms of Cullen

CHRONOLOGICAL TABLE OF TYPES AND SHAPES OF SHIELDS.

PLATE 37

Chronological Table of Types and Shapes of Shields

A shield may be depicted in any fashion and after any shape. There is no law upon the subject, and arms may be displayed, for instance, upon a banner, a parallelogram, a square, a circle or an oval. From the second half of the sixteenth century it became increasingly the case that the functional was sacrificed to the purely decorative. The shield generally was of wood, covered with linen or leather, the charges in relief or painted. After being decorated it would frequently be secured with metal clasps or studs

Fig 1. The original 'heater-shaped' shield (thirteenth century)

Fig 2. Shape of shield – fourteenth century

Fig 3. Shape of shield – fifteenth century

Fig 4. Shape of shield – French, fifteenth century

Fig 5. Shape of shield – fifteenth century

Fig 6. Type of shield – German, late fifteenth century

Fig 7. This type of shield is an example of the transition towards the 'Renaissance' shape of shield (late fifteenth century)

Fig 8. This shield incorporates a lance-rest to support a tilting spear (mid-fifteenth century)

Fig 9. Shield with lance-rest (sixteenth century)

Figs 10–12. Types of Renaissance shield (sixteenth century)

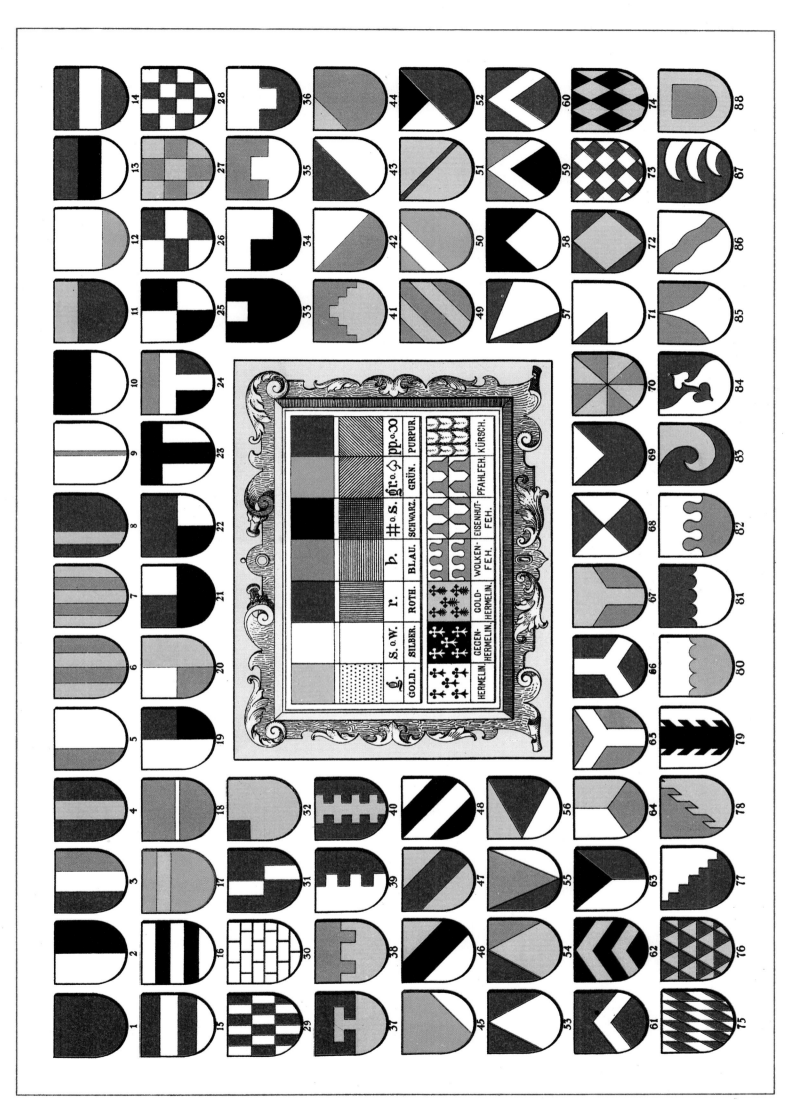

THE ORDINARIES AND LINES OF PARTITION.

PLATE 38

The Ordinaries and Lines of Partition

Every object used in heraldry is called a charge. The simplest charges are plain geometrical shapes and these are generally referred to as Ordinaries. Many are shown in this plate, such as the pale, 4, the fess, 14, the pile, 55, the pile reverse, 53, and the chevron, 61. Diminutives of the Ordinaries are used, such as palets, 7, and chevronels, 62. Also, the lines with which the Ordinaries or their diminutives are drawn need not be straight. Forty shows a pate bret and 86 a bend wavy. If a shield is divided in the direction of an Ordinary it is said to 'per' of that Ordinary. Thus 2 is per pale, 77 per bend indented and 38 per fess embattled. Here are also illustrated patterned fields, such as checky, 38, and lozengy, 73. In the centre panel it is shown (here in German) how colours are hatched, that is, shaded to indicate the tincture; thus gold is represented by dots and red by vertical lines. In the second row are detailed the various heraldic furs

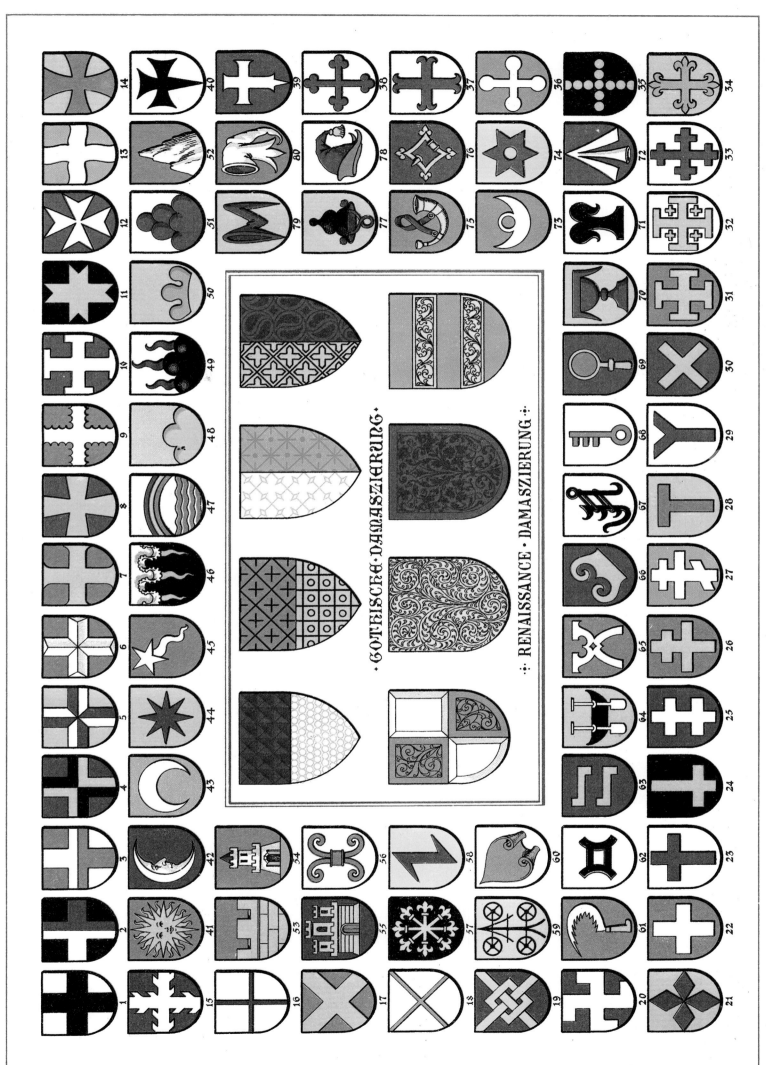

THE ORDINARIES AND OTHER HERALDIC CHARGES.

Printed at Stuttgart.

PLATE 39

The Ordinaries and Other Heraldic Charges
Some more Ordinaries, such as the cross, 1,
and the saltire, 17, are shown as well as
many variants of the cross – maltese, 12,
moline, 7, potent, 31, and Flory, 34. There
are also illustrated some other simple
charges, such as a sun in splendour, 41, a
mullet of eight points, 44, a maunch
(lady's sleeve), 79, an escarbuncle, 57, a
bugle-horn, 75, and a pheon, 72. The
centre panel illustrates diapering, that is,
the decoration of plain surfaces rather as
damask is decorated. This is not part of
the actual blazon of the arms but is purely
an artistic conceit

THE ARMORIAL BEARINGS OF—

(1) Sir Humphrey De Trafford, Bart.
(2) Wm. Speke, Esq. of Jordans, Co. Somerset.
(3) Dr A. Abercromby, of Cape Town.
(4) Sir Reginald Wingate, K.C.B., K.C.M.G.

(5) Thomas Bonar, Co. Kent—Matriculated 1812
(6) Arthur Fitz Herbert Wright, Esq. of Aldecar Hall.
(7) Theodore Napier, Esq. of Balmanno, Edinburgh.
(8) Lind, of Croydon and Oporto.